Indescribable.
A love letter.

Julieann Wallace

Indescribable - *a love letter*
© Julieann Wallace, 2025

Typeset by King's Ink Publishing in Adobe Garamond Pro font size 13, Silly Hand Script size 21
Kingsinkpublishing@outlook.com

The moral right of the author to be identified as the author of this work has been asserted.
This is a work of heart. Names of people are real.
All rights reserved. No part of this book may be reproduced or transmitted by any person or entity (including AI, Google, Amazon or similar organisation), in any form or by any means, electronic or mechanical, including photocopying, recording, scanning or by any format, storage and retrieval system, without prior permission in writing from the publisher.

Bible verses from The Holy Bible, New International Version* NIV* Copyright
©1973,1978,1984, 2011 by Biblica Inc.* Used by permission. All rights reserved worldwide.

All errors belong to the author.
ISBNs: 978-0-9923557-4-6 (hardcover) 978-0-9943982-6-0 (paperback) 978-0-9945366-9-3 (eBook)

Cover design by King's Ink Publishing
Cover image crown: Zolotons, flowers: Nata789
Interior art: Various 123rf, Adobe Stock - *HA - Human Art.*
earth - Wasanchy, heart - Shumo4ka, baby - Viktoriia, teardrop - Phatharaporn,
stars - WhataWin, Jesus - pronoia, Jesus - Iaroslav, angel - Nikolettamuhari, crown - LilVector

 *Julieann is a mum of three, Grams of one, writer, artist, teacher, and Christian, who tries not to scare her cat, Claude Monet, or her mini dachshund, Pablo Picasso, with her terrible cello playing. She was eight-years-old when she first heard the gentle voice of God, telling her to share with her brother (what a gift!). As a grown-up, she often hears the word 'trust' from God in her mind. Julieann is forever thankful to God who carries her through the storms, and she loves nothing more than to read the Word of God, and fall into worship of Jesus and our Heavenly Father. www.julieannwallaceauthor.com*

To my Heavenly Father, with all my heart.

Dear Lord,

Here I am with pen and paper, in our sacred garden where we talk.
Just You and me, surrounded by Your flowers, breathtaking and fragrant.
You, accepting me. Just as I am. And I'm so thankful.

I'm overcome.

I'm bursting with overwhelming emotion and my tears want to fall. I have no words as I inhale that sacred breath You gift me. It's just… *it's just too much…*

I exhale. I have no eloquent, silver-tongued words like a scholar to offer You, to write and to read to You with a whisper of deep love on the breeze.

It's just me, Lord. With a God-shaped heart and a profound adoration for You.

It's the work of Your hands, Lord, that gets me.
Your fingerprints. Over all of creation. Over the heavens and the earth. Over me.

And I'm undone.

I exalt Thee. 𝄞 ♪

I'm overcome, Lord.

By how wide and how long and how high and how deep Your love is.
That unbreakable, committed love that nothing can change. Or extinguish.
And my chin, Lord, it trembles at the knowledge that You choose me. No matter what.

I cry.

My tears tumble. I have no virtuoso, a soulful voice like a singer to offer You, the sound melodious, floating and swirling and scribing my love for You in the sky.

It's just me. With a quiet voice bursting with worship for You,
who honours You with all that I am.

It's Your love, Lord, that gets me.
That gracious, faithful, merciful love. That tender, kind, unchanging love.
That everlasting, unfailing, loyal love. For me. For humankind.

I could sing of Your love forever.

I exalt Thee. 𝄞♪

I'm overcome, Lord.

Filled with the deepest gratitude for that safe place I can go to, inside of me.
To reach out to You. To talk to You. To let my tears fall. To praise You.

And to *pray*.

I cry.

I lift my hands to You. I have no skill like a carpenter to offer You, to build You
a place of worship for people to gather in Your mighty name. To praise You.

It's just me. Who treasures every moment I spend with You, wherever I am.

You see me, Lord. My inner beauty. My gratitude and praise.
And my ugly, internal blemishes I try to hide from You.

You hear me, Lord. Mumbled and tear-filled. Distressed and pleading.
Thankful and sing-songy and filled with gratitude for You.

And You love me. No matter my past.
You renew me. You wash me with forgiveness and bathe me in Your eternal, perfect love.

It's Your approachability, Lord, that gets me. Even in Your unfathomable greatness.
Your invitation to sit at Your table. To be adopted by You.
And it's Your patience, Lord. Your compassion. Your tender concern for me.

Thank You for answering my prayers in Your perfect timing.

I exalt Thee. 🎵

And I'm overcome, Lord.

Falling to pieces at the profound knowledge that You knew me before I was born. That You knit me together in my mother's womb, fearfully and wonderfully made. And... You knew me by name.

I cry.

I place my hand over my heart. I have no majestic flowers in a stunning bouquet like a florist to offer You, the extravagant blooms a floral delight of perfumes, the colours breathtaking and luminous, spreading joy to all to shout of my love for You.

It's just me. Who cherishes You with all that I am, with wild flowers picked from a field, just for You.

It's the miracle of life, Lord, the sanctity, that gets me. It's Your blessing. It's Your face shining upon me. It's Your graciousness, and the peace You give.

Please accept my offer of myself back to You. An act of love.

Oh, Lord. 𝄞 ♫

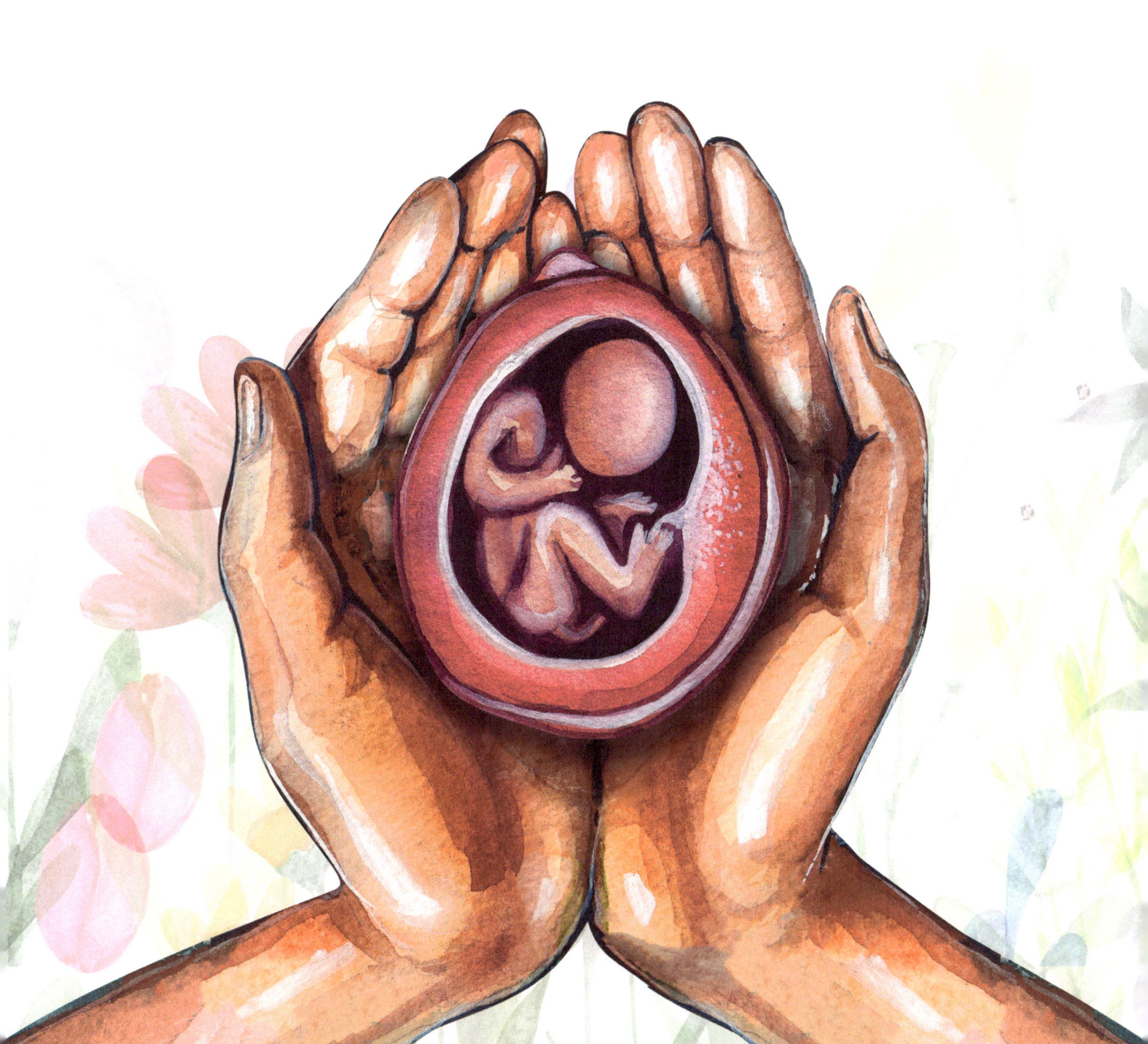

I'm overcome, Lord.

You see my tears and bottle them.
You see my struggle, my brokenness, my heart-wrenching moments...
My helplessness. My rejection. My despair.

My worship in the unbearable storm.

I cry.

I wipe away my tear. I have no controlled breath like a glassmith to offer You, creating lachrymatory bottles of every shape and colour to catch tears of grief, sealing them with Your knowing and understanding and love and compassion.

It's just me, with a broken hallelujah. Who depends on You with every breath I take.

It's my walk in life with You, Lord, knowing that I'm never alone that gets me.
It's Your patience, Your compassion, Your tender concern for me, and the hope You give that lifts me. Your healing.

Thank You for shining Your light in the darkness.
Thank You for healing my brokenness.
Thank You for holding my hand. Always.

I exalt Thee.

I'm overcome, Lord.

It's in the quietness after the setting of the sun when I look up,
lost in the glorious night sky, struggling to breathe as I consider the power of Your creation.
I'm overcome that You placed the stars in the heavens and You know them by name.
And those breathtaking auroras, Lord... the heavens declare Your glory!

I cry.

And I cover my face. I have no colour palette to paint like an artist to offer You, to use line and shape and form, repetition and emphasis and balance, to show Your greatness on a canvas signed with my love for You for all to see.

It's just me, Lord. Who is thankful beyond measure, with simple finger-paintings of You and me.

It's Your immeasurable power displayed in the night sky for all to see, Lord, that gets me.
It's Your signature, Your intelligence, Your mysterious nature, Your display of Your vast love for humankind.

And this... Your desire being that no one should perish, but all should be saved.

I exalt Thee. 𝄞 ♪

And I'm overwhelmed, Lord.

And it's because of Your indescribable gift. *Jesus*.

I inhale deeply. I have no gift to bring that's fit for a King. No gold, frankincense or myrrh like the Magi to offer You, Lord, not even a drum.

It's just me. With a heart for Jesus.

My throat tightens. His life. His human body. His human heart. His human mind. His human wills—one divine, one human. Without sin.

His marvellous, wonderful love.

I cry.

It's that You sent Your son, Lord, that gets me.
The perfect imprint of Your essence. Revealing You to me, and Your deep love for humanity.
And the love of Jesus, Lord... His compassion. His healing. His calling me by name.

Jesus is more than I ever deserve, God.
He walked upon the earth, for us, Lord. Undeserving us.
And this... He is a King, serving, instead of being served.

Unimaginable.

Jesus...
His death. I cry out with deep sorrow.

I exhale. ## His death...

It's the sacrifice He made for me, Lord, that gets me.
His obedience. His love. His passion.

Thank You for choosing the cross, Jesus. You didn't have to do it. But You did.
Thank You for suffering the immense agony and unbearable torture,
Your body beaten and broken. You didn't have to do it. But You did.
I'm overwhelmed and shattered by what they did to You, and my heart screams...
You didn't have to do it... but You did.

I cry.

Thank You Jesus, for Your precious blood poured out for me.
Thank You for Your profound, unfathomable love.
Thank You for finishing the work You set out to do,
fulfilling more than three hundred prophecies in the Old Testament.
And You breathed Your last breath on the cross, but Sunday was coming.

His resurrection...

On the third day, You rose, Jesus, as prophesied.
And You were seen by more than five hundred people in the days after.
My beautiful Saviour.

Thank You that by Your blood I'm forgiven.
I'll look forward to seeing You on that appointed day.

I cry...

I'm overcome.

The seen and the unseen.
The angels, God. Magnifying Your grandeur.
Your messengers. Sent to protect and proclaim, to help humankind.
Comforters, who will carry me to Your presence after my last breath.
You never forsake me.

I cry.

I close my eyes. I have no distinguished voice like an orator to offer You, words carefully chosen and curated, perfectly articulated and fluent, proclaiming my love for You.

It's just me. Who embraces You with all that I am, with whispers of hearts and thank yous and mispronounced words.

It's Your attention to my life, watching over me, Lord, that gets me.
Your deliverance. To that place prepared for me when I'm clothed with immortality.
And it's the imagining, Lord. Of Your divine holiness and incomprehensible power.
And me, humbly bowing down with the angels, singing Your praise and glory.

I weep.

I exalt Thee. 𝄞 ♫

I'm overcome.

And it's because of You, Lord. And Your pursuit of me.
You strengthen me. You renew me. You lift me when I fall.

I bow my head. I have no physical gift like an athlete to offer You, to run a race with
agility and speed and strength, leaving a blazing, golden trail of acknowledgement
of You before the crowd.

It's just me. Who bows down to You, straightening my imperishable crown of life,
that tilts and wobbles as I stumble, collecting Your glimmers and hope
and encouragement on my fingertips on my life journey. I couldn't do this without You.

It's Your presence, Lord, that gets me.
It's Your forgiveness. Your guidance. Your love for me.

And Your *Holy Spirit*... there are no words... I'm beyond thankful.

And this.
Our undeserved favour.

Grace.

Never earned, but freely given.
Thank You is never enough.

Please accept my eternal love for You, Lord, with all my *heart* and with all my soul
and with all my mind.

Oh, Lord. 𝄞 ♫

I cry.

Let everything that has breath, praise the Lord...

I'm bursting with overwhelming emotion and my tears fall, Lord.
I look down. I've written no words on paper, just a love letter to You on my heart.
You are simply...

Indescribable.

I'm on my knees.
Soli Deo Gloria.
Glory to God alone.

And Lord, I *pray*, that humankind fully comprehends their breath,
and the deep knowledge of it that transcends all understanding.

And I *pray*, that You Lord, *bless* all people and keep them;
make Your face shine on them and be *gracious* to them;
and that You turn Your face toward them, and give them *peace*.

In Jesus' name, Amen.

Scripture to accompany pages

Creation

Romans 1:20 For since the creation of the world God's invisible qualities – his eternal power and divine nature – have been clearly seen, being understood from what has been made, so that people are without excuse.

God's love

Ephesians 3:17-19 17 So that Christ may dwell in your hearts through faith. And I pray that you, being rooted and established in love, 18 may have power, together with all the Lord's holy people, to grasp how wide and long and high and deep is the love of Christ, 19 and to know this love that surpasses knowledge—that you may be filled to the measure of all the fullness of God.

Prayer

Philippians 4:6 Do not be anxious about anything, but in everything by prayer and supplication with thanksgiving let your requests be made known to God.
1 Thessalonians 5:16-18 Rejoice always, pray without ceasing, give thanks in all circumstances; for this is the will of God in Christ Jesus for you.
Romans 8:26 Likewise the Spirit helps us in our weakness. For we do not know what to pray for as we ought, but the Spirit himself intercedes for us with groanings too deep for words.

Fearfully and Wonderfully Made

Psalm 139:16 You saw me before I was born. Every day of my life was recorded in your book. Every moment was laid out before a single day had passed.
Psalm 139:13-14 For you formed my inward parts; you knitted me together in my mother's womb. I praise you, for I am fearfully and wonderfully made. Wonderful are your works; my soul knows it very well.

Tears

Psalm 56:8 You keep track of all my sorrows. You have collected all my tears in your bottle. You have recorded each one in your book.
Psalm 119:105 Your word is a lamp for my feet, a light on my path.
Hebrews 4:13 Nothing in all creation is hidden from God's sight.

Universe

Psalm 147:4 He determines the number of the stars and calls them each by name.
Psalm 19: 1-4 The heavens declare the glory of God; the skies proclaim the work of his hands. Day after day they pour forth speech; night after night they reveal knowledge. They have no speech, they use no words; no sound is heard from them. Yet their voice goes out into all the earth, their words to the ends of the world.
Luke 12:7 God knows how many hairs you have on your head. Do not be afraid.

Jesus

2 Corinthians 9:15 Thanks be to God for his indescribable gift!

Jesus' return

Revelation 1:7 Look, he is coming with the clouds, and every eye will see him,
even those who pierced him; and all peoples on earth will mourn because of him. So shall it be! Amen.
Matthew 24:36 But about that day or hour no one knows, not even the angels in heaven, nor the Son, but only the Father.

Angels

Psalms 91:11 For he will command his angels concerning you to guard you in all your ways;
Luke 2:13-14 And suddenly there was with the angel a multitude of the heavenly host praising God, and saying, glory to God in the highest, and on earth peace, good will toward men.
Colossians 1:16 For in him all things were created: things in heaven and on earth, visible and invisible, whether thrones or powers or rulers or authorities; all things have been created through him and for him.
John 14:2 In my Father's house are many mansions: if it were not so, I would have told you. I go to prepare a place for you.

Grace

2 Timothy 1:9 He has saved us and called us to a holy life—not because of anything we have done but because of his own purpose and grace. This grace was given us in Christ Jesus before the beginning of time.

www.ingramcontent.com/pod-product-compliance
Lightning Source LLC
Chambersburg PA
CBHW041443010526
44118CB00003B/163